For David

Here's some of the
bart art ever!

love.

Dad

LORENZO DE' MEDICI   MEDICI CHAPEL, FLORENCE

DEDICATED TO PETER KRASNOW, ARTIST, AND TO ROSE
HIS WIFE AND BIOGRAPHER

WORLD RIGHTS RESERVED BY ERNEST RABOFF AND GEMINI SMITH, INC.

LIBRARY OF CONGRESS CATALOGUE CARD NO. 71-139055

ISBN Trade: 0-385-07517-0
Library: 0-385-01998-X
PRINTED IN JAPAN BY TOPPAN

MICHELANGELO
BUONARROTI

By Ernest Raboff

ART
FOR
CHILDREN

A GEMINI SMITH BOOK

EDITED BY BRADLEY SMITH

PUBLISHED BY
DOUBLEDAY & CO., INC.

GARDEN CITY, NEW YORK

MICHELANGELO WAS BORN NEARLY 500 YEARS AGO IN CAPRESE, ITALY, ON MARCH 6, 1475.

HIS FATHER, LUDOVICI DI LEONARDO DI BUONARROTI, WAS ACTING MAGISTRATE OF THE TOWN. AFTER MICHELANGELO'S BIRTH THE FAMILY RETURNED HOME TO FLORENCE.

AT THE AGE OF 13 THE YOUTH WAS APPRENTICED TO THE WELL KNOWN ARTIST GHIRLANDAIO AND FROM HIM LEARNED THE ART OF MURAL PAINTING. AFTER ONE YEAR'S APPRENTICESHIP MICHELANGELO WAS INVITED BY LORENZO DE' MEDICI (CALLED "THE MAGNIFICENT"), RULER OF FLORENCE, TO STUDY AND WORK IN THE SCHOOL OF SCULPTURE HE HAD FOUNDED IN THE PALACE GARDENS.

HIS PATRON, LORENZO, DIED WHEN MICHELANGELO WAS 17. FROM THAT DAY ON HE WORKED INDEPENDENTLY FOR MANY OF THE RULERS AND RELIGIOUS LEADERS OF FLORENCE, BOLOGNA, AND ROME. AT THE AGE OF 24 HIS SCULPTURE CALLED THE "PIETA," OF THE MADONNA AND JESUS, MADE HIM FAMOUS. LATER HE WAS TO PAINT HIS CONCEPT OF THE CREATION OF THE WORLD ON THE CEILING OF ROME'S SISTINE CHAPEL.

FROM HIS NOBLE MIND AND CREATIVE HANDS CAME MASTERPIECE AFTER MASTERPIECE. MICHELANGELO WORKED AS PAINTER, SCULPTOR, ARCHITECT, AND POET UNTIL THE AGE OF ALMOST 90 WHEN HE DIED IN ROME ON FEBRUARY 18, 1564.

PORTRAIT OF THE ARTIST BY ERNEST RABOFF

MICHELANGELO IS QUOTED BY HIS FRIEND, GIANNOTTI, AS SAYING, "I HAVE ALWAYS TAKEN DELIGHT IN CONVERSING WITH LEARNED PERSONS..."

"WHENEVER I SEE SOMEONE WHO IS GOOD FOR SOMETHING, WHO SHOWS SOME POWER OF THE MIND, WHO CAN DO OR SAY SOMETHING BETTER THAN THE OTHERS, I AM COMPELLED TO FALL IN LOVE WITH HIM..."

ANOTHER WRITER, BERTONI, SAID, "MICHELANGELO DID NOT HAVE A LITERARY MAN'S STYLE, NOR ANY WORDS THAT WERE NOT HIS OWN, ALL HIS OWN, THAT IS, ROOTED IN HIS SOUL..."

MICHELANGELO'S LETTERS ARE FILLED WITH NOBLE THOUGHTS AND GOOD ADVICE. "MEN ARE WORTH MORE THAN MONEY." "GOING SLOWLY YOU MAKE FEWER MISTAKES..."

PIER SODERINI KNEW HIM AS: "A FINE YOUTH AND IN HIS CRAFT UNIQUE IN ITALY, PERHAPS IN THE WHOLE UNIVERSE.

HE IS OF SUCH NATURE THAT WITH FAIR WORDS AND KINDNESS ...HE WILL DO ANYTHING..."

PIETA   DUOMO, FLORENCE

"THE HOLY FAMILY" (CALLED THE DONI TONDO) WAS PAINTED TO HONOR THE MARRIAGE OF AGNOLO DONI. UNTIL THIS WORK MICHELANGELO WAS KNOWN PRIMARILY FOR HIS SCULPTURE. ON THE SIDE OF A SKETCH FOR THIS PAINTING, THE 29 YEAR OLD ARTIST WROTE, "WHO WOULD EVER SAY THAT THIS WORK WAS BY MY HAND?"

IN THIS OIL PAINTING, THE HOLY FAMILY SEEMS CARVED OUT OF STONE. THE BACKGROUND IS PAINTED AS A SEPARATE MURAL MAKING A HUMAN SETTING FOR THE HOLY MOTHER, FATHER AND CHILD.

THE GLOBAL SHAPE OF THE PAINTING ENCOMPASSES BOTH HEAVEN AND EARTH.

MADONNA, CHILD AND SAINT JOHN, BRITISH MUSEUM, LONDON

DONI TONDO   UFFIZI GALLERY, FLORENCE

"MOSES", ONE OF MICHELANGELO'S MOST IMPRESSIVE WORKS, TOOK FOUR YEARS TO CARVE FROM A HUGE BLOCK OF MARBLE.

THIS WORK REQUIRED YEARS OF STUDY, INCLUDING THE COPYING OF ANCIENT GREEK AND ROMAN SCULPTURE. YET THE ARTIST GAVE HIS OWN PERSONALITY AND PHILOSOPHY TO THE CARVING.

MOSES, LAW-GIVER AND RECEIVER OF THE TEN COMMANDMENTS (SHOWN UNDER HIS ARM), WAS THE LEADER OF HIS PEOPLE.

HIS HORNS ARE LIKE ANTENNAS TAKING IN WISDOM FROM THE HEAVENS.

CARVED OWL

HIS FACE SEEMS LIKE A LANDSCAPE. THE EYES ARE LIGHTS — THE SUN AND THE MOON WATCHFUL DAY AND NIGHT. HIS BROW AND NOSE ARE PROTECTIVE MOUNTAIN RANGES. HIS MOUTH IS A WELL, FILLED WITH WISE WORDS, AND HIS BEARD, A GARDEN OF VINES. THE DEEP LINES ARE FURROWS PLOWED BY CONCERN FOR HIS PEOPLE. MOSES' BODY, IN THE PRIME OF LIFE, IS A FORTRESS OF STRENGTH.

PORTRAIT OF ANDREA QUARATESI, BRITISH MUSEUM

MOSES   CHURCH OF SAN PIETRO IN VINCOLI, ROME

"THE ERYTHRAEAN SIBYL" WAS ONE OF THE TWELVE FEMALE PROPHETS CALLED SIBYLS, WHO IN THE AGES BEFORE CHRISTIANITY, FORETOLD THE FUTURE. MICHELANGELO PAINTED FIVE SUCH SIBYLS ALONG THE CEILING OF THE SISTINE CHAPEL IN THE VATICAN.

SHE IS A GODDESS-LIKE FIGURE OF CALMNESS AND STRENGTH. THE ARTIST PAINTED HER AS HAVING BOTH PURPOSE AND STATURE. IT WAS SHE WHO PREDICTED THE LAST JUDGMENT OF MANKIND, THE SUBJECT OF MICHELANGELO'S FAMOUS MURAL ON THE ALTAR WALL OF THE VATICAN CHAPEL.

HER FACE IS ROUND. HER EYE GAZES AT HER BOOK OF PROPHECIES. HER MOUTH IS TENDER. HER BRAIDED HAIR AND THE RIM OF HER COLORFUL HEADDRESS FOLLOW THE SAME SOFT LINES AS THE GARMENTS THAT DRAPE SOFTLY AROUND HER BODY IN SWIRLS OF WHITE, BLUE, GOLD AND PURPLE.

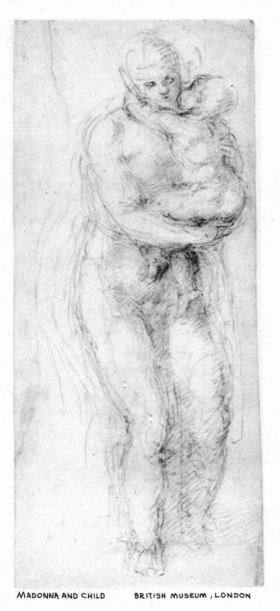

MADONNA AND CHILD   BRITISH MUSEUM, LONDON

ERYTHRAEAN SIBYL   SISTINE CHAPEL, ROME

"ST. PROCULUS", THE STATUE OF A DETERMINED YOUNG CHRISTIAN, WAS CREATED FOR THE TOMB OF SAINT DOMINICK WHEN MICHELANGELO, AN EQUALLY DETERMINED YOUTH, WAS ONLY 19 YEARS OLD. HERE WE SEE A FACE THAT IS RESOLUTE AND A BODY POISED TO MEET LIFE'S CHALLENGES.

FIFTY YEARS AFTER FINISHING THIS SCULPTURE, MICHELANGELO WROTE: "... PAINTING AND SCULPTURE ARE ONE AND THE SAME THING... EVERY PAINTER SHOULD NOT FAIL TO DO SCULPTURE AS WELL AS PAINTING; AND LIKEWISE, THE SCULPTOR. I MEAN BY SCULPTURE THAT WHICH IS DONE BY TAKING AWAY; THAT WHICH IS DONE BY ADDING IS LIKE PAINTING."

WE CAN ALMOST SEE THIS STURDY MUSCULAR BODY ALIVE AND MOVING BENEATH ITS MARBLE CLOTHING.

ST. PROCULUS   SAN DOMENICO, BOLOGNA

DETAIL, HEADS FOR THE JUDGEMENT   BRITISH MUSEUM, LONDON

"THE DELPHIC SIBYL" IN ANCIENT GREEK MYTHOLOGY WAS THE MOST FAMOUS TELLER OF FORTUNES. SHE WAS THE VOICE OF APOLLO, THE GREEK GOD OF MUSIC, POETRY, PROPHECY AND MEDICINE.

MICHELANGELO IN THIS DETAIL FROM HIS PAINTING IN THE SISTINE CHAPEL, SHOWS US THIS HANDSOME WOMAN HOLDING A PROPHETIC SCROLL IN HER RAISED LEFT HAND WHILE HER EYES GAZE PAST US INTO THE FUTURE.

THE FOUR COLORS USED BY MICHELANGELO IN HER GARMENTS COULD REPRESENT THE EARTH, FIRE, WATER AND AIR — THE KNOWN ELEMENTS OF LIFE ON THIS PLANET.

PERHAPS THE CHILDREN BEHIND HER ARE READING HER BOOK TO DISCOVER THEIR OWN PROPHETIC FUTURES.

THE DELPHIC SIBYL   SISTINE CHAPEL, ROME

"VIRGIN OF THE STAIRS", A MARBLE RELIEF, IS BELIEVED TO HAVE BEEN CREATED BY MICHELANGELO WHEN HE WAS 16 YEARS OLD. HE ONCE SAID, "AS A BABY I WAS NURSED BY A STONE-CUTTER'S WIFE AND I TOOK IN WITH MY NURSE'S MILK THE CHISELS AND THE HAMMERS I USE IN MY SCULPTURE."

IN THIS EARLY MASTERPIECE OF A YOUNG BOY NURSING, HE HAS GIVEN US THE MAN THE CHILD WILL BECOME IN THE MUSCULAR FORMS OF THE NECK, SHOULDERS, BACK AND ARM.

THE CALM FACE OF THE NURSING MOTHER PERHAPS GAZES INTO THE FUTURE OF HER CHILD.

DETAIL, VIRGIN OF THE STAIRS

VIRGIN OF THE STAIRS   CASA BUONARROTI, FLORENCE

"THE PROPHET JOEL"

IS ONE OF SEVEN ANCIENT HEBREW **SEERS** THAT MICHELANGELO PAINTED ON THE CEILING OF THE SISTINE CHAPEL. LIKE THE FIVE **SIBYLS**, THEY WERE CHARACTERS IN THE HISTORY OF WESTERN RELIGION. JOEL WAS A WRITER WHO WROTE THAT GOD WAS A KIND AND COMPASSIONATE BEING. THE ARTIST HAS SHOWN HIM AS A SERIOUS BUT GENTLE MAN. IT IS BELIEVED THAT A COLLEAGUE, DONATO BRAMANTE, THE ARCHITECT OF ST. PETER'S CATHEDRAL, WAS HIS MODEL FOR THIS PROPHET.

STUDIES FOR THE DOME AND LANTERN OF ST. PETER'S
TEYLER MUSEUM, HAARLEM

JOEL IS SHOWN READING FROM A SCROLL WHICH FORMS A LINE FROM ONE HAND TO THE OTHER ACROSS THE PAINTING. MICHELANGELO OFTEN DESIGNED HIS WORKS IN THE LINES OF A **CROSS** WITHIN A PYRAMID.

STUDIES OF A CAPITAL   CASA BUONARROTI, FLORENCE

PROPHET JOEL   SISTINE CHAPEL, ROME

"GUILIANO DE' MEDICI" WAS A MEMBER OF THE FAMOUS FAMILY THAT RULED FLORENCE, ITALY, FOR MANY YEARS. THIS MARBLE STATUE WAS CREATED FOR THE MEDICI CHAPEL.

GUILIANO HAS BEEN CARVED WEARING THE TUNIC OF A ROMAN GENERAL. THE **SCEPTER** OF COMMAND LIES GENTLY IN HIS SENSITIVE HANDS. THE THUMB AND FIRST FINGER OF HIS LEFT HAND HOLD A COIN. IT IS BELIEVED MICHELANGELO PUT IT THERE TO SHOW THE **MEDICI'S** RESPECT FOR AND GENEROSITY TOWARD ALL MEN OF THOUGHT, SCIENCE, LETTERS AND ART.

THE **ARTIST'S** GENIUS FOR USING HIS HAMMERS, CHISELS AND POLISHING STONES IS SHOWN IN THE DETAILS AND MOVEMENT OF THE STATUE'S GARMENT AND IN THE MUSCULAR FORMS OF THE BODY.

GUILIANO, WHO WAS ALSO A BROTHER OF POPE LEO X, IS PORTRAYED BY THIS MASTER SCULPTOR AS A MAN WHOSE INTELLIGENT FACE HAS BOTH

SENSITIVITY
AND
STRENGTH.

HEAD OF A BEARDED MAN   BRITISH MUSEUM

GUILIANO DE' MEDICI   CHURCH OF SAN LORENZO, FLORENCE

"THE PROPHET JOSIAH" AND HIS FAMILY FORM A TRIANGLE
FILLING A VAULT ON THE CEILING OF THE SISTINE CHAPEL.

THE **FATHER** IS THE BASE OF THE FAMILY PYRAMID.
THE MOTHER AND CHILD FORM THE TWO SIDES.

MICHELANGELO, LIKE ALL GREAT PAINTERS, USES LINES,
COLORS, FORMS AND SPACES AS A WRITER USES WORDS AND
PHRASES TO GIVE STRUCTURAL BEAUTY, DESIGN AND
MEANING TO HIS **THOUGHTS**.

THE MOTHER'S STRENGTH IS HIDDEN BENEATH THE FOLDS
OF HER WHITE VEIL AND HER **PURPLE** ROBE. SHE SITS
UPON HER GRASS GREEN SHAWL, ITS END CURLED IN
HER LAP, CLOSE TO THE **BROWN EARTH**. THE GOLD,
BLUE AND WHITE CLOTHING OF JOSIAH MIGHT REPRESENT
THE CHARACTER OF HIS SOUL, THE
BEAUTY OF HIS MIND AND THE
PEACEFUL NATURE OF HIS PERSONALITY.

THE MOTHER'S ARMS CLASP THE
CHILD IN A SOFT EMBRACE. THE
CHILD'S LEFT ARM CURLS IN A SOFT

ARC

FINDING SECURITY
BETWEEN
HIS RESTING PARENTS.

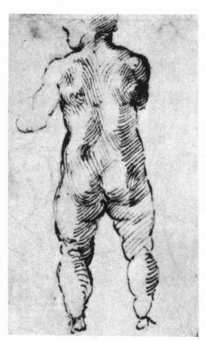

DETAIL FROM STUDIES OF CHERUBS
BRITISH MUSEUM, LONDON

PROPHET JOSIAH   SISTINE CHAPEL, ROME

RHYMES (1511)

"THE PROPHET ISAIAH" WAS A HEBREW SEER ABLE TO LOOK INTO THE FUTURE.

MICHELANGELO BUONARROTI WAS A STUDENT OF THE BIBLE. HE USED ITS STORIES AND ITS PEOPLE FOR HIS PAINTING AND SCULPTURE.

IN THE BOOK WHICH ISAIAH HOLDS OPEN WITH HIS RIGHT HAND IT IS WRITTEN: "...OUT OF THEIR GLOOM AND DARKNESS THE EYES OF THE BLIND SHALL SEE." LATER IN THE SAME VERSE HE SAYS: "IN QUIETNESS AND TRUST THERE SHALL BE STRENGTH". FOR MICHELANGELO THERE WAS DEEP MEANING IN THE PROPHET'S WORDS.

BOOKS, WHICH ARE SEEN IN MANY OF MICHELANGELO'S WORKS, BROUGHT HIM FAME AS A SCHOLAR AND POET.

HERE, ISAIAH TURNS FROM HIS BOOK TO LISTEN TO A CHILD.

RHYMES (AFTER 1546)

PROPHET ISAIAH   SISTINE CHAPEL, ROME

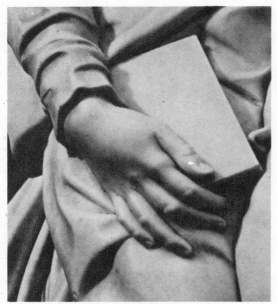

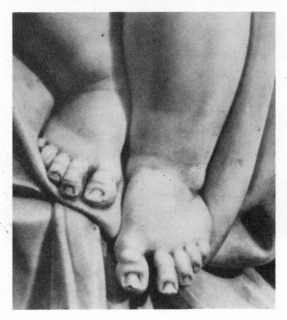

"THE BRUGES MADONNA"
IS A BEAUTIFUL EXAMPLE OF
THE 26 YEAR OLD MICHELANGELO'S
GENIUS. HIS ABILITY TO CREATE
ALMOST MAKES OUR EYES BELIEVE
THAT THIS MARBLE STATUE LIVES.
IF WE SHOULD TOUCH THE
MOTHER'S DRESS, IT SEEMS AS
THOUGH IT WOULD MOVE BENEATH
OUR FINGERS.

THE MADONNA'S FACE IS CALM
AND THOUGHTFUL. IT GLOWS LIKE
A MOON ABOVE THE PYRAMID OF
HER BODY. HER GRACEFUL
ARMS FORM THE SIDES OF THE
PYRAMID. THE LINE THAT CURVES
FROM HER RIGHT HAND TO THE
CHILD'S FOREARM, AND THEN
CONTINUES TO THE MOTHER'S
LEFT HAND FORMS THE BASE
OF THIS TRIANGULAR DESIGN.

THE BOY'S HEAD AND TORSO
DECORATE ONE SIDE OF THIS
PYRAMID ; THE MOTHER'S
DRESS THE OTHER.

DETAILS FROM "THE BRUGES MADONNA"

BRUGES MADONNA   CATHEDRAL OF NOTRE DAME, PARIS

"THE PROPHET ZACHARIAS" WAS THE FIRST PROPHET THAT MICHELANGELO PAINTED ON THE WALL OF THE SISTINE CHAPEL.

POPE JULIUS II, WHO BROUGHT MICHELANGELO TO ROME, IS SAID TO HAVE BEEN THE MODEL FOR THIS POWERFUL PORTRAIT.

DETAIL, THE PROPHET ZACHARIUS

THE CLOSE-CROPPED HAIR, MAJESTIC WHITE BEARD, AND THE LINED FACE OF THE PROPHET ARE THOSE OF A MAN WISE WITH AGE.

HIS FIRM HANDS LEAF THROUGH HIS BOOK AS THOUGH SEARCHING FOR AN IMPORTANT LESSON TO READ TO THE YOUNG STUDENTS WHO PEER OVER HIS SHOULDER.

THE PROPHET'S FLOWING GARMENTS FORM A SOLID BASE AROUND HIS SEATED FIGURE. HIS HEAD IS CENTERED ABOVE THE GOLDEN ARC MADE BY HIS RIGHT ARM.

DETAIL OF SIBYL AND OTHER STUDIES
DETROIT INSTITUTE OF ART

PROPHET ZACHARIAS   SISTINE CHAPEL, ROME